Gold! Gold! Gold!

Lalie Harcourt & Ricki Wortzman

Illustrated by
Susan Shaw Russell

⌐ᗡ Dominie Press, Inc.

I want gold.
Gold! Gold! Gold!

These are white.
I want gold.
Gold! Gold! Gold!

These are brown.
These are white.
I want gold.
Gold! Gold! Gold!

These are the gold ones I want!
Gold! Gold! Gold!